What's wrong with being a Skunk?

by **MIRIAM SCHLEIN**   illustrated by **RAY CRUZ**

Four Winds Press · New York

Library of Congress Cataloging in Publication Data
Schlein, Miriam.
  What's wrong with being a skunk?

  SUMMARY: Describes the habits and characteristics of several types
of skunks revealing some unusual facts about them.
  1. Skunks—Juvenile literature. [1. Skunks]
  I. Cruz, Ray, illus. II. Title.
QL737.C25S28   599′.74447   73-88078

Published by Four Winds Press
A Division of Scholastic Magazines, Inc., New York, N.Y.

Text copyright © 1974 by Miriam Schlein
Illustrations copyright © 1974 by Ray Cruz

1 2 3 4 5 78 77 76 75 74

Sometimes, when someone has done something very
nasty to you, something mean and rotten and unfair,
you might say:

"YOU'RE A REAL SKUNK!"

Why do you say that?
What's so bad about skunks?

Here's a skunk. He—or she—is not mean and nasty. He hardly ever fights with other skunks, the way people fight with other people. He is playful and really very good-natured. He is about as big as a cat—from about eleven to fifteen inches long, not counting his tail. He walks around slowly, very relaxed.

He may be walking down a path, and if he meets a bear
coming in the other direction, he just stands there,
and waits for the bear to get out of *his* way.
And do you know something? The bear will get out of the
skunk's way. Even though he is many times bigger
and stronger than the skunk.
Why is this?

It is because the skunk has a very special kind of weapon that the bear doesn't like. It is the weapon of STINK.

He doesn't use it to be spiteful or mean. He only uses it when he feels he is in real danger. He uses it to save his life. Even so, he doesn't make a sneak attack. He gives plenty of warning.

This is what happens.

A skunk meets someone — a person or another animal — that he thinks might hurt him, or even kill him.

He — or she — stands there, very still.

If you don't go away, he stamps on the ground with his foot. He's warning you: GO AWAY! Sometimes he chatters his teeth, or he growls.

If you still don't go away, he raises his bushy tail. All except the tip of it which still hangs limp. This is another warning. You still have time to get away. If you don't, if you come closer to him, he will lift the very tip of his tail up stiff.

He fires!

He – or she – shoots out an oily yellow liquid that smells terrible. He can shoot two streams of it at the same time. It comes from two glands in his rump, near his tail, but he can shoot it at you while he is still facing you. He just twists his rump around and shoots the stinky stuff at you without even getting any of it on his own fur.

He can squirt it a distance of ten feet with good aim. He aims for your eyes. And too bad if he hits you because his fluid is more than just very stinky. If it hits you in the eye, you are blinded for a while. It burns your skin, too.

This stinky liquid is the skunk's main weapon, and it's a good one. And the skunk really has to depend on it, because aside from biting or scratching, there's not much else he can do to protect himself. He can't run away from danger too well, because he's not very fast. The Striped Skunk—the most common kind of skunk in the United States and Canada, and the one we see most often—can't even climb a tree for safety. He can swim a bit, if he has to. (The smaller Spotted Skunk *can* climb a tree.)

But there is one serious problem that the skunk has with his weapon. He can shoot only five rounds of it. Then he has no more. He has to wait a few days for his scent glands to fill up again. He is, in a way, out of ammunition. He has to be careful where he goes and who he meets at a time like that.

Not many animals will attack a skunk. Horned owls will —possibly because they have no sense of smell. And sometimes a skunk will be attacked and killed by a very hungry fox or bobcat. They have to be desperate to go after a skunk. But sometimes they are. And then the skunk's weapon doesn't do him any good.

There is another time when his stinky weapon doesn't help him — or her — at all. At night, on his wanderings, sometimes he must cross a road. He sees something coming at him, but it is not his habit to run from danger, so he just stands his ground. And he is hit by a car.

Skunk is a night-animal. He — or she — sleeps in the day, but is active at night, prowling around for food. Sometimes we call people who stay up a lot at night "night-owls," because owls are out at night. Maybe we could also call them "night-skunks" for the same reason.

Are you a night-skunk?

A skunk is not a fussy eater. He eats lots of different things. He eats fruit and corn. He likes to eat frogs, and turtle eggs, and bird eggs, too. He catches and eats moles and chipmunks and shrews and even rabbits. A skunk knows how to eat bees and wasps and a bee's honey without even getting stung!

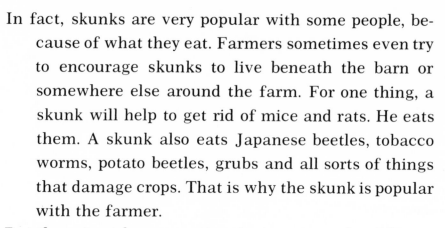

In fact, skunks are very popular with some people, because of what they eat. Farmers sometimes even try to encourage skunks to live beneath the barn or somewhere else around the farm. For one thing, a skunk will help to get rid of mice and rats. He eats them. A skunk also eats Japanese beetles, tobacco worms, potato beetles, grubs and all sorts of things that damage crops. That is why the skunk is popular with the farmer.

But there is at least one time he is not popular. That is when he raids the henhouse.

After a summer of eating grasshoppers and crickets and mice and wasps and eggs and all the other things, he —or she—is fat and full of food and ready for the winter, when food is not easy to find. What he has to do now is find or make a warm, safe home for winter.

Sometimes he uses the old deserted burrow of a wood-chuck or a badger. Or he can go into a cave, or find a snug spot in a stone wall or beneath a barn. Or he can dig his own new tunnel a few feet long. At the end of this tunnel, he scoops out a nice room which he fills with dried grass and leaves.

Sometimes skunks use a tunnel that has already been built by another animal—maybe an opossum or a woodchuck. They just build their own private room off this tunnel. This usually seems to be all right with the other animal. It's an animal-apartment-house.

Sometimes, lots of skunks live together — some mothers and their young, and other male and female skunks. They're not a family. They do it for company. It's a skunk-commune.

Here they are. Up above is snow and sleet. Everything is frozen. But the skunks are snug in their den.

While they sleep, they just live off the layers of fat they've accumulated during summer and fall. But when there is a mild day, once in a while skunks will get up, leave the den, and go looking around for some food above the ground. There is not too much to find in winter — no fruit, vegetables, or insects. So they eat small animals for food — perhaps a mouse or a mole. Then they come back to the den.

Around February the male and female skunks mate. This is the only time a skunk might sometimes shoot his Stink at another skunk. That happens when two males are fighting over the same female skunk. And even at this time, it is still very rare for a skunk to use his special weapon against another skunk.

About nine weeks later, in the spring, the baby skunks are born. Each mother skunk usually has between four and seven babies. She nurses them. They are tiny. They weigh less than one ounce. When they are born, their eyes are closed. They can't see. They are wrinkled and have no hair. But even then, they have on their skin black-and-white markings similar to the markings they will have on their fur later on.

Three weeks go by before they open their eyes. During this time, their furry skunk fur is beginning to grow. When they are about five weeks old, they are able to follow their mother to the outside world. There they go, all in a line behind her. Now she will begin to teach them how and where to find food for themselves. A few weeks after this, they no longer have to drink milk from their mother. They can live on regular skunk food.

Through the summer, the young skunks stay with their mother. But in the fall, they already know enough and are grown enough to go off on their own, if they want to.

Do they want to? Some do. And some don't.

Most young skunks go off on their own and find burrows for themselves, or move in with some other different skunks. A few young skunks stay with their own mothers for the next winter season.

Here he—or she—is. A skunk—a Striped Skunk—in his first autumn. He can rely on himself now. He doesn't have to depend on his mother. He has a small, pointy head, tiny bright eyes, rounded hairy ears. He has short legs; he stands low to the ground. He is wider at the hips than at the shoulders. He is about eighteen inches long, not counting his tail, and he weighs about eight pounds.

He has a long, thick, hairy coat. It is black or dark brown. Between his eyes is a narrow white stripe. There is a white patch on top of his head, and along his back are two white stripes, one on each side.

There's no mistaking him. He's a skunk.

This is exactly why the skunk has that very bold, unusual coloring on his fur. So that there is no mistaking him! So that other animals do *not* attack him, mistaking him for another small furry animal. If this happened, they would both be sorry. But then it would be too late. With this kind of fur coloring, a skunk doesn't look like anything but a skunk. It would be hard to mistake him, even at night, for another animal.

All skunks do not look exactly alike. The Striped Skunk is the most common skunk in the United States and Canada. There are more of them than the other kinds.

There is another kind of skunk called the Spotted Skunk. He is smaller than the Striped Skunk, and on his back there is more white coloring, which is broken up into lines and spots. The Spotted Skunk is more rare than the Striped Skunk. There are fewer of them.

A Spotted Skunk is the only kind of skunk that can climb trees. He can also stand on his front paws. Sometimes he does this for fun. Mostly he does it as a warning. He means: GO AWAY. If you don't, then he will start walking toward you on his front paws. Because of his small size, the Spotted Skunk can get a better "shot" standing in that way.

If you ever see a skunk walking toward you on his front paws, like an acrobat, it may look like a wonderful trick—but don't sit around and applaud. Just leave. Very quietly.

There is a kind of skunk called the Hooded Skunk, similar to the Striped Skunk except that his two stripes are farther apart from each other, and there are some black hairs mixed in with the white hairs on his back.

The skunk called the Pygmy Skunk is a type of Spotted Skunk.

There is another kind of skunk that has a nose like a hog. He is called the Hog-nosed Skunk.

Striped Skunks are found in southern Canada, the United States and northern Mexico. Spotted Skunks are found from southern Canada, through most of the United States and Mexico, down to Central America. Hooded Skunks are found in the southwestern United States down through Central America.

The Hog-nosed Skunk can also be seen in the southwest United States. And he is the only kind of skunk that lives in South America. With his blunt, hairless snout, he roots and snuffles in the ground for insects. The Hog-nosed Skunk is the largest kind of skunk. He can be as big as twenty inches long.

Skunks are found only in the Americas. They are not found anywhere else in the world.

If you are ever in Africa, you might see an animal that *looks* like a skunk, and *acts* like a skunk, and *smells* like a skunk. But it is not a skunk. It is a zorilla.

Even though they resemble each other very closely, they are two different kinds of animals. A skunk is not a zorilla, and a zorilla is not a skunk. They developed entirely separately and they are not related to each other. It is like two people who look very much like each other, and might almost be taken for twins. They are look-alikes. But they are not even twins. They can be absolute strangers. That's the way it is with the skunk and the zorilla.

It is not easy to know exactly how long a life a skunk that is living in the wild has. It is thought that they sometimes live to be about six years old. Six summers fat and furry, eating eggs and crickets and wasps. Six winters snug in the den, when the world outside is too cold. Mating in winter, and babies in spring, and in the summer helping them grow and teaching them what skunks have to know. Then, they are grown-up skunks, knowing that animals ten times their size are afraid of their own special weapon.

What's wrong with being a skunk?